Empty but useful in the HAND OF GOD

Amarachi Angel Osisioma Alaike

Empty but useful in The Hand of God

Copyright © 2022 Amarachi Angel Osisioma Alaike

All rights reserved. No part of this book may be reproduced or transmitted in any form or by any means without the written permission of the author.

Scriptures marked KJV are taken from the KING JAMES VERSION (KJV): KING JAMES VERSION, public domain.

Scripture taken from the New King James Version®. Copyright © 1982 by Thomas Nelson. Used by permission. All rights reserved.

Scripture quotations marked (NIV) are taken from the Holy Bible, New International Version®, NIV®. Copyright © 1973, 1978, 1984, 2011 by Biblica, Inc.™ Used by permission of Zondervan.

All rights reserved worldwide. www.zondervan.com. The "NIV" and "New International Version" are trademarks registered in the United States Patent and Trademark Office by Biblica, Inc.™. Scriptures marked AMP are taken from the AMPLIFIED BIBLE (AMP): Scripture taken from the AMPLIFIED® BIBLE, Copyright © 1954, 1958, 1962, 1964, 1965, 1987 by the Lockman Foundation Used by Permission. (www.Lockman.org)

Published by:
Eleviv Publishing Group
Centerville, OH 45458
info@elevivpublishing.com
www.elevivpublishing.com

ISBN: 978-1-952744-68-6 (PB)
  978-1-952744-70-9 (E-book)

Printed in the United States of America

Dedication

I dedicate this book to God Almighty, The Creator of heaven and earth, and The Father of our Lord Jesus Christ. The One who has preserved me from my mother's womb fought for me and chose a nobody like me to do His work. To Him alone be all the Glory and Honour forever and ever.

Acknowledgement

I would like to appreciate my husband, the man behind the scenes supporting me in the work. You know I love you and appreciate you, Mr. Victor Alaike. I would also like to acknowledge and appreciate my mentor, Apostle Queen Belema Abili of Queen Belemzy's Ministries, School of Power. Thank you so much for obeying God and for the many times God has used you to be a blessing to us.

Table of Contents

Dedication

Acknowledgment

Foreword

Preface

Introduction

Chapter 1 **Aunty M**... 8

Chapter 2 **My Foster Mother**... 18

Chapter 3 **American Returnee**... 30

Chapter 4 **My Biological Mother Comes Calling**... 38

Chapter 5 **London, Here I Come!**... 49

Chapter 6 **Giving My Life to Jesus**... 57

Chapter 7 **Stumbling into destiny fulfillment**... 87

Chapter 8 **Prayer Points**... 96

Chapter 9 **Conclusion**... 102

A Letter of Thanksgiving to God

Introduction

My name is Amarachi Angel Osisioma Alaike. I was born in Owerri, the capital of Imo state, in the southeastern part of Nigeria. I was raised mainly by my foster mother, madam Angelina Mbam, who was popularly nicknamed 'Madam Do-good.' She had several nicknames at the time, but this particular one stuck to her more than the others. She was the one I grew up to know as my mother, and she never once gave me a reason to believe otherwise.

The first four years of my life were not very eventful. It was my period of innocence when I knew next to nothing about the difference between birth parents and foster parents. I never knew that Madam Angelina Mbam was not the one who gave birth to me; neither did it occur to me that there was no fatherly figure in my life. Living with the popular Madam Do-good was like any other child in the neighborhood living with their mother. Little did I know that separation from my foster mother and many difficulties lay ahead.

Soon, the whole rhetoric of my life changed for a less palatable fortune. The joy and innocence I enjoyed were ripped off, and I was left to live a life of pain and regret, even at such an early stage. When I was around five years old, my foster mum, Angelina, took me to Enugu to live with her sister, aunty M. The reason for taking me to her sister was not immediately apparent then, but it was a significant turning point in my life. At that point, life began for me. The next few years of my life made me see some ugly sides of life.

Chapter 1

Aunty M

Aunty M was a civil servant who was very strict and disciplined in every way. My foster mum had thought that because her sister possessed these qualities of strictness and discipline, she would be best placed to help me stay focused in school. The rest of my story would tell if she was wrong or right. My foster mother probably thought I was getting pampered, and her way of tackling that was to take me to her sister for some time.

Aunty M was a well-known disciplinarian in the quarters where we lived. People feared her. Children my age always make sure they steer clear of her because of her no-nonsense attitude. Their perception of what aunty M was, rubbed off on the way kids around related to me. While a few thought I was protected, many pitied me and the invisible prison cage I carried around. Some even avoid playing with me because of aunty M.

Whenever I made a mistake or did something wrong, aunty M would flog me mercilessly. The society where I grew up saw nothing wrong in flogging, but aunty M took hers to a rare height in dealing with me. Beating me for her was a daily necessity regardless of my efforts to stay out of her trouble. The first few days I lived with her were filled with threats and signs of trouble ahead; it soon developed into full-scale beating that began to increase by the day.

Sometimes, she would beat me with a pestle or a piece of wood. She would grab virtually anything in sight to hit me. There was little I could do at that early stage of helplessness and innocence. To make matters worse, her maltreatment of me got to a stage where she would strip me naked and put pepper in my eyes or private part. The beating will continue along with the agony of pepper in vital areas of my body. It was a terrible ordeal for someone, especially at such a young age. Her reasons for beating me so much were often ridiculously flimsy that, in hindsight, I still wonder at her reasoning and behaviour towards such a little child.

I believe her lifestyle and attitude toward people around her heavily impacted her relationships with the opposite sex. It is, however, an area I would rather not delve into without her consent. People saw her for what she was and related to her based on what they saw. Many people outrightly avoided her, and even at my young age at the time, I could easily tell that people avoided her. That people avoided her meant little to me; what I found to be of concern was that some avoided me too because of her. Some adults would not let their children play with me because of aunty M. It was a tough time in my young life.

While struggling to make sense of all I was going through, little did I know that another unfortunate event was around the corner. Even though I was not enjoying the kind of treatment aunty M was dishing out, I would gladly persevere with her than have her drag another innocent person into my predicament.

She accused our neighbor of sleeping with me when I was eight to ten. The man she blatantly accused was a respectable family man with children, some of whom were older than me. Even though some people in the neighborhood avoided me because of her, this man was one of the few who played with me as a man would do with any child in the area. He used to look at me with pity, knowing what I was going through. Even an occasional greeting and smile from him was always a welcomed relief. Aunty M accusing such a person of sleeping with me was shocking.

The accusation was false, yet aunty M reported him to the police. I remember vividly how scared I was at the police station. The truth was that the man was innocent, but I was too afraid to say so because I knew the beating I would get if I dared counter aunty M's statement to the police. Therefore, I consented to make an innocent man suffer. My inability to confess to the truth that the man was innocent was the final nail in his coffin. With tears in my eyes, I consented to toe the same line of lies as aunty Maria. I was not crying because I was molested but rather because an innocent man was wrongly accused of molesting me, and there was nothing I could do to vindicate him.

This event played on my mind for a very long time and badly affected my relationship with the children of the innocent man. Even other children who heard what happened also began to keep me at arm's length. My aunty M, however, could not be bothered to care about such sentiment.

Aunty M was indeed very troublesome. She was the reference person in the quarters for comparison when people talked about troublemaking and bad attitudes. At a point, neighbors no longer feel restricted from talking about her and her poor attitude even in my presence.

People noticed how she physically assaulted me and sometimes tried to step in to stop her from beating me, but her response was always so rude and abusive that the intercessors gave up trying to advise her. There was no such thing as a child welfare body around at the time, and so there was no authority for neighbors or concerned persons to report to.

Aunty M would make me wash and rinse her clothes at least six times and would beat me if she was not satisfied. Often, she would not be satisfied after rinsing her clothes several times and would still punish me for wasting water. I remember how I struggled at the time to wash her heavy adult clothes. It was difficult for me to discern at that young age where I had to begin washing the clothes as I had to wash with bare hands and not with a washing machine. I would struggle to wring the water out of her clothes with my tiny hands, unable to muster enough strength to squeeze out the water from the washed clothes effectively.

There was hardly any house chore that seemed too much for me to do for aunty M. I virtually did everything from cooking and cleaning to running to the market to obtain one thing or another. She would often spit on the floor and say to me, "if my spit dries by the time you go to the market and come back, I will beat you," and many a time, she did. She would make me work for hours, and at times I wondered if she did not understand that I was tired after such long hours of working. My sad expression and the slouched figure did little to deter her from seeming determined to turn me into a domestic working donkey. Laughter and gaiety were strange to me during that period; the only time I would enjoy such was watching TV shows such as Tom and Jerry or Tales by Moonlight.

She would lock me inside the house for hours and, sometimes, for the whole day. Sometimes she would go out with the key, locking me inside. I would only peep out the window at the little of the outside world I could see through such a restricted view. Aunty M had no care or consideration for the possibility of such an emergency as a fire outbreak. It was comfortable for her to lock me in while she went to her place of work. I was always sad and lonely.

Sometimes I saw other children celebrating their birthdays, but I never enjoyed such a luxury with Aunty M. I never knew the experience of wearing special clothes for a special occasion. Even if Aunty M were to arrange such a day of celebration for me, not one of the children who were afraid of her would even show up to the occasion. If it were the case that Aunty M didn't have the money to do anything for me on my Birthday, I would have understood, but the truth is she was a civil servant who was doing very well in her career and thus doing very well for herself. She wasn't married, she had no children, and even the house we were living in was given to her by the government. So, you see, that was not the case. My Aunty M was never apologetic about anything she put me through. I can't recall her ever saying sorry or being remorseful about anything that concerned me. She never told me she loved me once while I stayed with her. Perhaps she never experienced such while growing up, and she naturally passed this over to me.

At the time, I never questioned the origins of my birth but was yearning for my foster mother to come to pick me up because I was suffering, and every day my food became tears. The was no joy; there was no happiness. I barely laughed; I barely smiled.

Whenever aunty M locked me indoors, it was never with the motive of having me relax and enjoy myself. Instead, she would make a ridiculously long list of house chores for me to do. Sometimes I run about within the house to complete all the activities lined up for me to do before the return of almighty aunty M. Occasionally, some kids in the quarters would talk to me, but we would only speak through the window because I was locked in.

I lived in a state of constant fear of being reprimanded by her because her punishment was always severe. People knew about these things, which added to her notoriety in our neighborhood.

Aunty M would go to work at around 10 a.m. and return home between 4:30 p.m. and 5 p.m. After some time, she thought it best for me to stay at a neighbor's house after school, which was a welcomed development as I did not have to run through a list of activities before, she arrived from work or stayed lonely indoors all day long. At this time, she began observing me closely because of rumors of intimate interactions between the boys and girls in our quarters. This may have created suspicion in her mind about my conduct at the time. Her suspicion did not surprise me; after all, she had wrongly accused a family man in our quarters of sleeping with me.

In her limited wisdom, aunty M would check my private part most days after she arrived from work to see if any man had had sex with me. She did not know that when I would stay at our neighbor's house, my neighbor's sister, who was much older than me, would usually abuse me sexually and warn me not to tell anyone. And because I was so scared of aunty M, I dared not tell her. Thus, I lived in a state of fear from two ends -- the fear of being molested at my neighbor's house after school and being flogged by aunty M if she got to find out. Therefore, I concluded that one pain was better than suffering two. I still feel the psychological effect of the series of molestation to some extent, even now.

Back to aunty M. I was petrified of her flogging. When I reminisce about it, I see her beating me like an adult. I remember how much pain I would feel whenever she taught me my ABC, 123, or any other subject. When I gave the incorrect answer, she would beat me without regard for my age. To her, it was a criminal offense to miss her questions, even at that age. What she did not know was that most of the questions I missed were out of fear and inability to concentrate rather than being unable to figure out what the answer should be.

Unfortunately, some boys who lived near our quarters began to sleep with me around that time. However, this was consensual. At my age, I knew nothing and had no close confidant to run to. It was not difficult for the boys to lure me into the sinful act of sex with some vain promises. The abuse at my neighbor's house and my intimacy with the boys continued until I was 10 or 11.

At this time, Madam Angelina, my foster mother, paid us a visit in Enugu. With tears streaming down my face, I quickly took that opportunity to tell her that I wanted to leave Enugu for good. She noticed a mark on the side of my face, which I believe drove her to conclude that she needed to take me back with her to Aba, where she lived. If not for the mark on my face, which hinted at the hellish experience I had been through, my foster mother would probably have left me back in Enugu to continue drowning in the sea of suffering.

Even though my foster mother meant well, she did not know how much of a damaged commodity she was taking back with her. There were some of the experiences of my past five years I could not voice out to even her. She took the bold step of taking me with her to a better place and with better care, but the truth is, so much damage had already been done in my life.

While some of these damages were erased quickly, some were so deeply etched on my subconscious mind that even today, they still play on my mind. The physical injuries, like scars on my skin, were relatively easy to deal with. Some even disappeared over time, but the emotional and psychological damages remained in my head. Some of the things I was exposed to, like sex with boys and at such an early age range, were not things that could be easily wiped off my memory. Once a child is exposed to such, the tendency is to continue in such a mess despite a location change. Except such child undergoes deliverance, and God heals them. The location change might have taken off some situations and acts, but it did not take the memories and lewd desires off my mind.

All the same, leaving Enugu was a huge relief for me. It was a welcomed development and one I was willing to hold on to, even if it meant letting go of everything else that might have given me temporary relief back in Enugu. The day I left Enugu for Aba with my foster mother was one of the happiest days of my life. The joy of escaping from aunty M, the opportunity to be with my foster mother again, and the expectation of a better life ahead were overwhelming. I fought back the tears as I looked forward to a life closer to normal regardless of all I had been through.

I packed my few belongings, not daring to look at aunty M for fear of a sudden change in plan between the two women. Despite my few belongings, it was as if I had taken forever to get ready for the escape trip. The disappointment in my foster mother's eyes could be seen after another round of discussion between her and aunty M. I was not interested in the subject of their discussion or the outcome. All I wanted was to escape from aunty M, and I was glad I got just that.

Chapter 2

My Foster Mother

My foster mum was a strong and industrious woman. She was a woman leader who influenced happenings on the street where we lived. Many people respected her, including the police. She was also called 'Margaret Thatcher' or 'Iron Lady' in reference to the stern and first female prime minister of the UK. This was because of her no-nonsense character and strength.

Although my foster mother could be very firm, she was not as callous as her sister, aunty M. She is not as emotionally hardened and indifferent to the suffering of others as her sister. To that, I was so grateful. It took a while before I began to see my foster mum as tough. I must confess that my foster mother was lenient in how she handled me.

I grew up during the era of the "Bakassi Boys."

These were an aggressive and self-assured gang of twelve men who carried guns, knives, and a plethora of charms. They meted out jungle justice supposedly on behalf of the people. I remember how they looked; huge, vicious, with faces rivaling a terrible thunderstorm. Their leader was comparatively small but was manifestly the most fetish amongst them. He would wear a live tortoise as a neckless around his neck as he paraded the street flanked by his hefty subordinates.

They would apprehend criminals and kill them immediately on the street. They determined who was guilty by using their charms. Whenever their knife would shine red, it would mean that the individual in question was guilty, according to the rumors. Immediately upon that signal, they would slaughter the man or woman on the street. Many times, they would first parade the condemned person, who would be bleeding from the severe beatings he had received, around the streets. It was a strong warning to others and a form of mockery for the guilty. They would either cut their head off or burn them alive. I witnessed their judgments many times. They were self-appointed judges and warriors who would often track down notorious criminals. They were ruthless and seemingly committed to their cause which they were convinced was righteous.

The people largely supported the activities of the Bakassi Boys because they rose to prominence at a time of high crime rate in Aba. It got so bad that it became apparent that the police could not contain the criminals who were having field days stealing and even killing innocent victims. The local heroes began their activities like a vigilante group before expanding into something else. Their actions soon spread to other areas around Aba. Their area of dominance continued to spread, living trails of blood behind them.

Surprisingly, the police avoid them, giving them a free hand to operate throughout the state and even beyond. Even though their activities pull a huge crowd, no police officer shows up to ask any questions. Such was the power the Bakassi boys wielded in the city of Aba in those days.

My foster mum owned a restaurant/bar which the Bakassi Boys patronized often. They became good customers, and sometimes, my mother gave them drinks on the house. I remember when these boys would pass by on the street, and people would run and shut their businesses to avoid them. But that was not the case with Angelina, my fearless foster mum. Often when they were around, she would come out to hail them, and they would, in return, greet her warmly, calling her by her nickname "Madam Do-Good!"

My foster mum's relationship with the Bakassi Boys boosted her standing in the community. Many wondered how she managed to relate so closely and freely with such dangerous people without falling foul of their judgment one day. Not only that, but several people around the neighborhood also began to attach other sentiments to the relationship between my foster mother and the Bakassi Boys. They felt there must be some deeper relationship between her and the men, that she was maybe operating as a secret agent for them. All the speculations only made the status of madam Do-good grow in the area. That was not true because, naturally, my foster mum was a sociable person.

I was always nervous when I served the vicious-looking Bakassi Boys when they visited our restaurant because I used to steal money from my foster mother to buy snacks and clothes. Therefore, I was afraid their blade would one day flash red and out me as a thief. So, I learned to pray to God for forgiveness to avoid being exposed by the charms of the Bakassi Boys, who execute judgment without mercy. My hands would shake when I was in their midst as I sold them cigarettes and would even get asked to light the cigarettes for them. Thankfully, their blade never turned red, and I was never caught for any of my petty crimes, at least not yet, and not by the men of the Bakassi Boys vigilante group.

  Madam Angelina's bar and restaurant also had two adjoining rooms that she rented out for a hundred naira for half an hour for any purpose the customer needed. We sold many things. Food, drinks, Akara (grounded beans that people would buy in the morning or evening), sweet potatoes, pepper sauce, plantain, cigarettes, herbal concoctions made of alcohol, and the bark of different kinds of trees, as well as some other local ingredients and palm wine. I remember customers would come to me and ask for alcohol with roots for 'washing and setting' just before they would take their lovers to one of the side rooms to sleep with them. What they meant by 'washing and setting' was that they needed something to erect their manhood before they went in and did their business with the women. Some of the concoctions my foster mother sold were local aphrodisiacs, and many of her customers believed strongly in them. Once a customer finished in the room, they would then come to me to ask for alcohol with roots that would help cleanse the semen from the body of the woman or for something that would prevent her from becoming pregnant. Such ignorance. At that age, I knew which concoction was meant for what function. All they needed was to tell me what functions they needed, and I would arrange the right concoction or mixture of concoctions for them.

    I was a little over eleven years old at the time, although I looked older than my age because my growth was quite precocious. I remember the foul smell from the room after the customers finished. I was exposed to many things from a young age—sex, alcohol, smoking, and the dirty banter characteristic of many bars. Even though I did not understand much of the dirty slang I heard every day at my initial stage of spending my days at the bar, with time, I soon understood and got used to them.

Soon after, I began getting involved in everything I heard about myself. I remember when I would sleep with a man, I would consume the same alcohol with roots to avoid pregnancy. That was the lifestyle of grown-up men and women, so I quickly picked up those habits. Nothing was off-limits for me.

Madam Angelina, also known as Madam Do-good, had her hands in many pies. She was a leader of the women association in the area and was involved in local politics. Consequently, she was often not in the restaurant when many things took place. I remember encountering a much older man who said he liked me and wanted to sleep with me. This was typical of the encounters I had with many men during that time and was just a function of that environment. Married men and women, who were cheating on their spouses, would bring their lovers to Madam Angelina's guest rooms which I helped to manage at times. I remember the customers I served always mentioned my maturity for my age.

They believed that I was fair game since I understood what was happening. Eventually, I entered sexual encounters with some customers who would frequent the restaurant. At first, when these men made their advances, I was hesitant and nervous. Often, I would not want to, but sometimes they would persuade me, and I would eventually yield to their advances. I remember how I felt deep down when I agreed. I did not want to, but I gave my consent anyway because I did not know how to say no. I cannot remember precisely when I began to take these things in their stride and saw them as usual, but it soon became a way of life, and I began to enjoy it.

The attention, the advances, and the intimacy became a norm for me. It became part of the clockwork of the day-to-day operation of my foster mother's restaurant. There was one man who used to patronize our restaurant every Sunday. If Madam Angelina were not with me that day, he would take out his manhood and touch himself while staring at me. When no customers were present, he would cajole me into caressing his private part. He would make me stroke it repeatedly and put my mouth on it if I had not resisted. He would then quickly put it away when a customer came in. I never told Madam Angelina, my foster mother, about these encounters. I did not know what she would think or how she would react.

It was not like I was innocent at the time, as I had a record of stealing that my foster mother later became aware of. Working in her restaurant, money was always passing through my hands, and my foster mother was selling many things. Aside from the food, drinks, and guest rooms, Madam Angelina also had a borehole. People would bring their buckets and jerry cans to buy water. Even though there were other boreholes around town, what made ours standout was the cleanliness of the environment that surrounded it.

So, money was always coming in, and I would sneakily pocket some to buy snacks at school or when I went out. For me, it was fun always to have money to spend and a sharp contrast to the kind of life I lived in Enugu. I did not give much thought to the source of the money or the danger of being caught stealing.

One day, one of the students at my school reported me to my teacher. She said she did not understand where I got all the money from. Those days I would go to school with a lot of money, buying all sorts of edibles. I bought some snacks, fruits, and so on, not because I needed them but because I could afford them. I also paid for other children who were there. It was my little way of showing relative opulence compared to other students my age.

The teacher reported me to the famous Madam Angelina, popularly known as madam Do-good. My foster mother wasted no time concluding that I was stealing from her, and she dealt with me.

Another time my foster mother noticed that some money was missing in her shop. She promptly suspected me as the culprit since she knew I had frequently stolen from her in the past; it was easy for her to beam her torch light of suspicion on me without hesitation. I remember she checked every article of my clothing from head to toe. When she could not find the money, out of frustration and a keen suspicion that the money was on me, she made me take off my clothes for a thorough search. Eventually, she found the missing money in my pant or sometimes my sock or school bag. It was another low point for me as the cloud of shame gathered again. I did not know what to say, and she dealt with me again.

As if that was not enough, there was also a time I got drunk. It was at a time when Madam Angelina, my foster mother, was preparing for the burial of her late father. She purchased some special alcoholic drink that was in a container. She put it in her room for safety. Unfortunately, I had access to her room. I would sneak to her room, lift the container and take a drink. I did this many times throughout the day until it was almost finished. Then suddenly I passed out. I did not know what had happened to me or when it happened. All I can remember was that I woke up in the afternoon the following day.

I was so intoxicated, I was told, to the extent that I had to be revived. When I woke up, I thought I had overslept, and I couldn't understand why. I was expecting my foster mum to beat me, but as I walked out to the front of the restaurant, I was greeted with a chilling glance from my foster mum as she was seated with her friend. To my surprise, she never touched me. I believe she was too shocked by the ordeal. I later heard mama say it was like an attack as if the devil wanted her to bury her father and me during the same period. This occurred when her father was at the mortuary and scheduled to be buried. I believe God brought me back to life. I couldn't explain what happened to me, but I Thank God. I had a record of misbehaviors and was unsure how my foster mother would react to the fact that I was also sleeping with men. Or rather, I was afraid she would disgrace me beyond what I could imagine.

I recall when Madam Angelina, my foster mother, would publicly embarrass me for one extreme offense. She would address my misbehavior in the restaurant while customers were present and call me 'onyeshi' (the Igbo word for thief) and tell everyone I was stealing. I could not bear the thought of my foster mother doing the same thing to me if she were to find out that I was also sleeping around. So, I felt it would be better to avoid the shame and not tell her, so my secret illicit sex with men of all shapes and sizes continued. I remember Madam Angelina would speak so well of some of her customers, sincerely taking them to be good men and genuine customers. Unknown to her, many men only came around because they wanted to sleep with me. I never felt like a victim, but at the same time, I was very young and did not feel like I had the power to refuse their advances. Though it was consensual, I now see that those men were taking advantage of a little girl.

I recall that while I was in Aba, I had three abortions. My foster mother was aware of the first one but had no knowledge of the other two. When my foster mum found out I was pregnant she was so disappointed. Men always wanted to sleep with me, and I, for whatever reason, was not going to refuse their advances. Instead, I saw their overtures as another opportunity for fun and excitement. From my experience, I can safely conclude that nymphomaniacs can be made rather than born.

It was the same situation in school, except the advances came more from fellow girls. It was a boarding school which made certain things more likely to happen. Admittedly, lesbianism was not something I took to. However, I had two sexual encounters with two girls, but I remember feeling disgusted after each session. I recollect that there was a girl who always told her classmates that she liked me. There was also the head girl who persistently asked me out that I kept turning down. She once heard me say, "I would never sleep with her." This angered her so much. Since that day, she seemed to look for an opportunity to get back at me for daring to refuse her advances despite her position and social standing in the school.

One night I decided to sleep at my then-boyfriend's place, which was at the other end of the boarding school premises. His father was the vice principal of the boarding school, so their family lived within the school premises. Unfortunately, I got caught. Sometimes before lights out in my boarding school, there was a roll call to see if everyone was in bed. Of course, I was absent that night when the roll call was carried out, which was how I got caught.

    The head girl took up my case when I returned the following morning. Somehow, maybe because I was not the only one engaging in such an ungodly act, my matter did not get to the ears of the school authority. Out of jealousy and anger, the head girl gave me one hundred and fifty strokes of the cane on my feet. Even though she made it paper, it was because of my escapade of the night before, but some of us understood it was because I refused her several advances of taking me to bed.

    My foster mother never got to hear about the whole ordeal. She had sent me to a boarding school in a bid to curb my excesses. She intended to clip my wings and subdue me, but it was a failed attempt. Rather than curb my immoral excesses by sending me to a boarding school, I was exposed to more immorality.

Chapter 3

American Returnee

The year 2001 was a bad one for me as my world came crashing down. It was another year of a significant low in my already topsy-turvy life. It all started when Madam Angelina's brother returned from America after thirty-three years abroad and was very hostile. That was when my life started spiraling downhill again. While I was growing up, there were times I heard people say in low tones that Madam Angelina was not my mother, but I ignored them for two reasons. Firstly, there was no proof, and secondly, my foster mother and I had a strange resemblance.

Madam Angelina had lost one of her eyes long before I came into her life. As a result, she used an artificial eye that she would always pop into the eye socket when she woke up in the morning. It looked like an animal's eye and was bigger than her natural eye. On the other hand, I had crossed or squinted eyes that people noticed and would sometimes mock me for. Some would say I had "four o'clock eyes." This affected my confidence, and I could not hold eye contact with people while speaking with them. So, when people looked at Madam Angelina and me, they always said we looked alike somehow. I never asked my foster mother how she lost her eye. I dare not. It was not the kind of question I was permitted to ask as it would be considered rude.

The final reason I ignored the voices that said that Madam Angelina was not my biological mother was that she never gave me any reason to believe I was not her daughter. She was good to me in her way. She even tolerated my excesses and handled them in her way.

But unfortunately, on that fateful day, her brother from America broke the news to me that Madam Angelina was not my biological mother. He had been hostile from the first day he arrived, throwing his weight about and making life miserable for everybody around him. His arrival shattered the peace of the compound where we lived. He would bark at everybody with his bloodshot eyes, and even when he smiled, it was with a sardonic expression. It was as if he had been looking for an opportunity to burst my bubble. His eyes would follow me about as I did my possible best to avoid him and his threatening glare. When his first opportunity to shatter my world came, he did not hold back; he seized the chance firmly. He looked straight into my cross-eyes and told me his sister was not my birth mother. There was no emotion in his eyes as he broke the news like a bottle containing a substance with a foul odor.

He also said that the surname I bore at the time, Okoro, was not my surname. Madam Angelina's brother also sarcastically advised me to ask his sister who my birth parents were. He further said in a very hostile tone that if I wanted to get married, he would not be the one to give me away because he might be committing an abomination. I assumed the abomination he was speaking of was based on breaches of cultural traditions.

So, one day in fear, I asked Madam Angelina who my biological parents were. She insisted that I was still her child even if she picked me from the gutter. She said with an air of finality that it did not matter what people might have been saying or what

I had heard; what mattered was that she was my mother. After that, it was difficult for me to press her any further.

My foster mother's brother continued reiterating that I did not belong to their family. He was busy shredding my already busted bubble and driving everybody else around to the wall.

One day, Madam Angelina's brother decided that we all should leave our then-home. He claimed that Madam Angelina did not have any right to the property because he was the only son of their late father, and that fact conferred on him the absolute right to all their father's properties. He then chased us out of our home, giving us no time to pack our things. Madam Angelina and I lost our belongings. She was only able to leave with the clothes she was wearing.

It was terrible, so awful. The whole compound and Madam Angelina's shop were claimed by her barking brother, who had decided to bite. We were forced to move to an uncompleted house after that. It was the last resort as the eviction happened too suddenly, and there was nowhere else to go. I was surprised to find out that a whole madam, Angelina, could be so caught unawares by such a catastrophic occurrence.

I recollect sleeping on a mattress on the floor while the construction of the house was taking place. On top of that, I was grappling with a troubling situation occasioned by the America returnee's revelation. The woman I had believed to be my mother all these years was not my mother, as her response to my confronting her was insufficient to allay my worries. However, such a troubling time was not suitable to press on with such a request about who my birth parents were.

During the eviction period and Madam Angelina's effort to stay put, her brother kept telling me that I needed to look for my parents. He kept hurling those ugly words at me, and each time he barked at me to look for my birth parents, it felt like weights were being dropped on my soul. I could hardly concentrate on the eviction problem going on around me. I felt dizzy and depressed hearing those words from the heartless brother of Madam Angelina. Not even his fake American accent could douse the hurt his words caused me. How I survived it all, I cannot tell. I was in a sad dream as Madam Angelina eventually left the compound, and I went with her. We ended up in the uncompleted building. Fortunately enough, Madam Angelina was able to plan for some builders who were her former customers to do a rush job of completing a section of the property for us to stay in.

After brooding over my situation for a while, with the double jeopardy that had befallen me, I felt I needed to decide the course of my life going forward. I felt that since I had no family and was getting no answers from my foster mother concerning my birth parents, I might as well live my life the way I wanted. I felt a strange sense of freedom to become wild and live my life the way I wanted. It was the devil himself whispering into my ears.

Madam Angelina's brother continued to make life hard for us. He would still come to the uncompleted building that had become our abode to shout at us. He kept threatening to throw us out of the uncompleted building as well. After his threats, a feeling of sorrow and resignation to fate enveloped me, and one day, he gave us an ultimatum to leave the uncompleted house we were living in. I thought the building belonged to my foster mother, but he argued that the proceeds from their late father's property that afforded us the uncompleted house was rightfully his. I could not fathom the depth of wickedness of the man as he stood in front of the uncompleted house shouting for the whole world to know that something was going on.

Beads of cold sweat broke out on my forehead. I had never been so distressed in my life. If I had been a legitimate child of their family, perhaps I would have been bold enough to fight back, or at least try to that effect. But there I was, nursing the harsh reality of my true relationship with my foster mother.

Also, seeing a whole madam Do-good, the "Iron lady," the only "Margaret Thatcher" of Aba, being rough handled and reduced to such pitiable fate further broke my spirit. I had never been so helpless and lost in my life.

Eventually, the self-acclaimed landlord allowed Madam Angelina and me to stay in the house, but he moved in with us. That was yet another ridiculous move from him, leaving the whole compound where we left some while ago and moving in with us in the uncompleted building. I later understood that he was on a mission.

While living with us, he made life intolerable for my foster mother and me. He would restate again and again that he owned the uncompleted house by virtue of his position as the only son of their late father. He leaned firmly on the absurdity of the culture of the land to pour untold torments on us. I watched as Madam Angelina began to wither away, changing from the lively madam Do-good we all used to know to an ordinary shadow of who she used to be. She withdrew deeper and deeper into her empty shell until there was no further depth to withdraw to.

The worse the situation got for my foster mother, the more worried I became. I knew something had to give. I knew we could not continue with the toxic situation for too long. Unfortunately, I was too powerless to steer the rudder of our fortune in a favourable direction.

Soon, Madam Angelina began to contemplate moving back to their father's house in the village. She needed some respite from her bully of a brother. She was broken beyond what even I thought possible. Of course, we all knew that there was always the possibility of her brother fighting her over the ownership of the less fanciful house of their father in the village. Still, we expected their father's kinsmen to protect Madam Angelina in the village.

I was bracing up for a life in a village. I understood that things would never be as rosy as they were in the city of Aba, at least before the arrival of Madam Angelina's brother. I thought of my suffering academics, the question mark over the issue of who my birth parents are and their location. My mind was befuddled with all those unpalatable thoughts.

My foster mother told me to move back to her sister's house in Enugu. The announcement of her decision came as a massive blow to me. I thought it was better to die than return to that hellish place. I stared at her in complete shock as the harsh reality of what was to come dawned on me. As the tears rolled down my face, I recalled all I went through in Enugu and how I thought I had escaped from aunty M for good. Then the thought of the wasted opportunities flooded in as well. I realized how miserable my life had been. All that kept me going was a tiny glimmer of hope that things might change for the better somewhere along the line, even if it meant running away to an unknown destination.

It was too easy for Madam Angelina to see the

turmoil in my mind. She made me understand that she wished fortune would smile on us. She did her best to convince me that her decision was the best for me then. I knew any act of resistance would only amount to piling more pressure on her already ragged mind. After all, caring for me so much was only a free will sacrifice on her part, as I now know.

Eventually, I left for Aunty M's place, and madam Angelina my foster mother, went to live in the village. At the time, communication was not as accessible as it is today. I didn't have a cell phone then, so I had no way of knowing how she fared. I was also preoccupied with my worries as I faced a familiar challenge that I would have gladly dodged if possible.

Chapter 4

My Biological Mother Comes Calling

The years rolled along quickly; it was soon the year 2004, my year of a significant turnaround. I had relocated to Enugu and lived with aunty M, who seemed not to be as hostile as she used to be, perhaps because of her age. I had grown more mature and aware of happenings around me; I was not the same little girl treated like a useless rag doll all those years ago.

However, my life was still severely affected by the return of my foster mother's brother. He took everything from my foster mother, madam Angelina and rendered us broke and helpless. Madam Angelina went from owning a property that had eight shops that she rented out, a restaurant, a borehole, and two guest rooms to having no income or a place to call her own. The unfortunate turn of events was a rude shock. As I look back today, I am glad my poor foster mother could weather through the storm.

When I arrived in Enugu, I met my Aunty M, who was older and not as strong as she used to be when I was much younger living with her. She was, however, very energetic to help. She asked me about my interests and if I would consider learning about I.T. (computer knowledge).

I was already in my late teen, with my education cut short. I had no formal training in any trade, so she knew a decision had to be taken concerning that sooner or later. I took a few days to settle into my new life, spending much of my time indoors while aunty M went to work.

After a few more days passed, aunty M felt that it was not a good idea for me to be in the house doing nothing while she was at work, so she made arrangements for me to enroll to study IT at a college. On getting to the college for inquiry, we were told that I needed certain documents from my former school before I could be enrolled in the program we had targeted. As a result, I had to return to Aba to obtain the required papers from my former school.

Back in Aba, I began to think about what I could

do with my life. I was not particularly interested in the program aunty M was planning for me. I stayed back in Aba for a while, squatting with my then-boyfriend and his family, who lived near mama and me in Aba. My life had become seemingly hopeless. So, I thought of going into prostitution to take care of myself. When I mistakenly mentioned my decision before my boyfriend at the time, he discouraged me. He said that no matter how hard things got, I should never contemplate prostitution. I felt ashamed of myself and decided to hold back on my shameful decision.

One fateful night something incredible happened. I was out with my boyfriend and his friends at a hotel bar near our house. It was not the first time we were hanging out together at that particular bar. Spending time drinking and eating with friends helped alleviate my worries, so I looked forward to such outings.

Spending time at the bar had become a routine with no unusual event except for the occasional brawls involving one or two drunk customers. Generally, it was always a good experience.

One fateful evening at the bar, a woman on

the phone came into the hotel and walked past us without a word of greeting. By what I firmly believe to be divine providence, I heard the woman's voice as she spoke on the phone, and I recall saying to my boyfriend that I liked the woman's voice. Shockingly, I found out later that she was my biological mother and that she was lodging at the same hotel.

The next day she went to my former home but found no one was around, so she reached out to my neighbour and told her who she was. She had been asking questions around, following some leads in an attempt to locate Madam Angelina and her long-lost daughter.

As madam Angelina my foster mother, had returned to the village to cool off from her brother's antagonistic behaviour, my neighbor asked my biological mother to come back in a few days to enable her to get in touch with us. I was beyond just happy when my former neighbor located me and explained things to me. My situation was so bad that I wanted my biological mother to quickly take me out of the mess. I was not even interested in doing too much investigation of my own about her claim; I was just grateful that someone had come forward to claim me and help me bear my burden.

You see, when my biological mother came looking for me, she eventually spoke to my neighbour. My neighbour, in turn, told her to leave her number with her in the event they were able to speak with my foster mum and me. The next day my neighbour reached out to me and explained these events, and from there, we scheduled a day we would be reunited.

When I was making my way to meet my mum, I was so excited. Many things went through my head. I felt hopeful that things would get better for me, and my biological mum was about to sweep me away and give me a better life. I was just happy after being without such for some time.

My mum and I met at my neighbour's house. We spoke, and she explained the circumstances surrounding why she had to leave me. After this, we arranged to go and see my foster mum in the village.

I understand she informed my father that she had traced my whereabouts, and he was surprisingly eager to meet me. He quickly planned to accompany her to meet me.

I was not the only one surprised by these events. My neighbour, who first became aware of all this directly from my biological mum, was also shocked and in almost disbelief. They had always known me as the daughter of Madam Angelina and never suspected differently.

I wouldn't be surprised if the things taking place gained the curiosity of neighbors and onlookers. My mother's dressing and look dripped luxury and comfort. That sent tongues wagging from the first day she showed up asking questions about me in the area. It was easy to tell she was not like the usual woman from that area and commanded some respect.

Ideally, the very traditional and conservative Aba people would have rained insults on such a woman who could abandon her daughter for many years. She would have been labeled an evil woman; some may even dare to spit on her body. She would not have been accepted. However, the case of my biological mother, madam O, was different. The aura of confidence around her and her look paid to whatever negative thought or plan anybody could have had about her.

Another interesting thing I observed was her gentle tone of voice. It seems to douse the flames of any judgemental anger anyone could have had towards her.

At the time, it never occurred to me to verify the claims of this woman who just showed up, stating that she was my mother. Nor did it occur that I may be in mortal danger of some kind. I was excited, eager, and willing to go wherever this woman took me. Perhaps this was how God wanted it, or maybe I was excited because I saw this as my only way out.

I remember when my mother and I first sat down to talk. She called me by my birth name that I had never heard until that moment, "Amarachi." It means the grace Of God. It was here that she began to narrate the story of the circumstances of my birth and the strange event that took place many years ago when she was trying to abort me. As soon as she started talking, narrating all that happened almost twenty years ago, my former neighbor's sitting room became quiet as we all listened to her with rapt attention. Even though her story revealed some faults on her part, surprisingly, nobody attacked her or called her names.

According to my mother, she became pregnant with me at fifteen and was certain that the pregnancy was a month old when she wanted to terminate it.

She went to a doctor who told her that she was three months gone and that she might die if she tried to terminate the pregnancy. That was a big shock to her. She was so sure about the date of my conception. So not being deterred by the doctor's words, she asked questions and soon found another doctor who might help with her quest. When she got to the doctor and was examined, she was told she was already more than three months old. The doctor also warned her that she would not only regret aborting the pregnancy but would most likely die along with the innocent baby growing in her abdomen. The doctor's words dampened her hope of getting rid of the pregnancy and made her settle for her fate. That was how God saved me in the womb.

According to my mother, she eventually agreed with the doctors to allow the pregnancy to survive to maturity and birth. When she finally gave birth to me, she decided to leave me with my father's mother so she could return to school. My father, too, was unable to look after me because he was already scheduled to go abroad on scholarship to study and was not prepared to suspend or cancel his trip to accommodate a child. They were both relatively young and inexperienced.

Neither were they ready to face the rigors of married life when they had not completed their educational pursuits or could run a home.

Eventually, my dad's sister handed me over to her friend, my foster mum, who then adopted me as her child—the years rolled by with my parents moving away from Aba to pursue their educational goals. I grew up knowing my foster mother as my mother with no memory of my birth parents.

God has a way of doing things. He has His way of making sure things come to pass, and whatever He had determined to do cannot be changed by man. Many years later, my biological mother married and tried unsuccessfully to have children for her husband. She had forgotten about me, assuming I was dead. She looked to raise children with her husband, which would have been the end to any hope of a reunion between us. She said that while she could not take in, she repeatedly had dreams of a baby crying and pulling her clothes. She figured this could be me because she had abandoned me some years earlier. So, she reached out to my father's family concerning my welfare, only to be told I was dead. However, the dreams didn't subside; they continued to the point that she had them every night. While this was happening, she was told by a man of God that she had a child somewhere. So, she then asked my Father's family if they could take her or show her where the burial place was so she could pray over the site so my soul could rest in peace. However, their responses to her seemed strange. They appeared not to be forthcoming concerning helping her locate the burial ground, and that's when my mother suspected foul play.

My mother complained to the village king, who reached out to my dad's family. After that, my dad's family finally revealed the truth and told my mum I was alive. This sparked a series of events that led to my birth mother meeting my dad's sister, who then directed her to where mama and I were living in Aba.

Once my biological mother and I were reunited, and after she explained all that happened during the time, she was pregnant with me. We agreed that my dad would accompany us to travel to the village to meet mama officially. Once we arrived, my biological mother and father began to explain to my foster mother that they were not here to take me from her but to send me to school, perhaps abroad, to give me a better life. After much discussion and some awkwardness during the meeting, things were concluded, and both parties seemed to understand. I couldn't tell what was happening within my foster mother then, but I'm sure that underneath her stern demeanor, there might have been some pain she felt with the scenario.

Soon after, I traveled to Lagos with my biological mum and was enrolled in a boarding school called Christland College. I had to start in Senior Secondary school one because I never passed my exams from that level back in my former school in Aba. Once enrolled, my mother traveled back to Holland, where she was based.

During school vacations, my mum's sister would pick me up, and I would stay with them for the holidays. It was a new world entirely for me. I felt like my complicated past was a mere figment of my imagination as I settled into my new life in Lagos. Even though I was perhaps the oldest in my class and way more exposed in some ways, I was determined to make the best of the lifeline life had thrown at me. Despite my precocious growth and well-developed body, I knuckled down to learn and did not hesitate to learn from people younger than me in my class.

During that time, my biological mother would travel to Nigeria during the festive period to visit and stay with us. Apart from my biological mother, I was also excited to have met my father. Before my birth mother came into my life, I had only a foster mum and no father figure in my life. So, I was always so happy whenever I was around my father. I would often call him every half an hour just to hear his voice and have him say good things to me. Sometimes when I was with friends, I would call him, showing off in their presence just to let them know I had a father. This may have seemed strange to those around me, but I didn't care. It was a new experience, and I loved the moment.

When I came to Lagos with my mum, we initially stayed in her house. I was so happy to be with her. She bought me decent clothes and designer stuff and always wanted me to look presentable around her friends. I did my best to act my part, seeing that her cycle class was high compared to what I had been used to back in the eastern part of the country. Lagos was the place to be. Beautiful sceneries, great places to visit, sophisticated fashion sense, the way of life in Lagos was far different from what was obtained in Aba. I was, however, eager to blend with the ways of the Lagosians.

I had my hands full all the time in Lagos. While not at school, my aunties and cousins from my mother's side would take me out to see places. While I was in Aba, I was only used to visiting bars and hotels for relaxation, but Lagos was different; there were eateries, cinemas, beaches, musical shows, and so on. Not only that, attending church in Lagos was entertainment. The music, the dancing steps, and the dressing of the several beautiful and handsome people in the church it was so much fun to be in Lagos.

On top of that, I constantly communicated with my dad, who ensured I lacked nothing. He would come down to see me whenever possible, which helped our bonding. Later my dad returned to London, where he lived with his wife and three children, my younger siblings. The thought of having younger siblings and the hope of meeting them one day was heart-warming. I could not help telling myself, "Welcome to the future."

Chapter 5

London, here I come!

Despite my effort in secondary school, I barely managed to finish without being tagged as a total failure. My background was not fantastic, and the standards in my new school were way higher than what I was used to. I always struggled in my academics. I had difficulty comprehending most subjects, so I never did well. Through scrupulous means, I did manage to graduate barely. I was going down the path of cheating, whether copying others or bringing my textbook to the exams.

In 2010, my dad arranged for me to travel to the United Kingdom to study. All the necessary arrangement was made, and my papers were sorted. I was so excited at the opportunity to study abroad, and my preparation was in top gear.

I was excited about what the future holds

as I envisioned a perfect scenario once abroad. I understood I came to study but was also looking forward to the change in environment.

So, I arrived in the United Kingdom, England. I could not hold back my excitement because of the weather, the people, and the architecture of the buildings. I was picked up from the airport, and my life in the United Kingdom began earnestly. I had no way of telling that it would end in premium tears before God's divine intervention.

I soon started school and found myself struggling. It seemed to me I was enrolled in the wrong subjects and found myself learning about things I had no prior experience with. I tried my best or something close to that. Unfortunately, I did not do well. I failed woefully. To my dad's surprise, I could not make it beyond the first year. I was so ashamed of myself and decided to try again. Unfortunately, my dad struggled financially and could not sponsor my re-enrollment back to university.

Even though I remained in the United Kingdom at my dad's house, I became unhappy. My younger siblings were going to school, and I would often be left in the house on my own. During that time, my life became monotonous. I would wake up, help around the house, watch TV, and sleep. I wanted more and didn't know what to do to change things. I was in a strange land; I had no friends and didn't understand the system. I felt stuck.

Meanwhile, my biological mother and I had fallen out. She wanted certain things to go her way and felt I was inclined more to my father's side than hers. It was not my fault. I probably wanted that fatherly figure in my life more, and the opportunity to be with him was difficult not to grab. I never made things easier; however, my mother and I had disagreements about other things, and eventually, compounded by her view about my favoritism, we finally stopped talking at a point.

I began to look for happiness in the wrong places. I started going out and not returning home till the following morning sometimes. I spent as much time as possible with my then boyfriend and sometimes his friends.

I eventually got a job at a cab office in Deptford. It was very low-paid work, below the minimum wage, because the owner knew I didn't have my documents. I was initially thrilled because it gave me a modicum of respect and independence. It afforded me the ability to buy my bus pass to move to and fro and continue to play a part in the weekly church activities that I often looked forward to.

My happiness at the Deptford cab office quickly disappeared. The owner began to make lustful advances toward me, and I often acquiesced to the ungodly banter. I did it because I felt I needed the job. I was also afraid of my immigration status, and the system in the UK was still alien to me. What also saddened me was that I knew that God was not pleased with the kind of dirty banter I had with the owner. He was a married man; nevertheless, I accommodated his behaviour. When no one was around, he would also try to touch me.

I eventually left and got a job from a lady running a clothing store and helped with money transfer customers. She was very good to me; she loved me like a daughter. When I told her I was leaving, I sensed the sadness that a mother would have for a daughter who is leaving home for the first time. Although a mother is sad, she knows that it's time and is still happy for her. When I left, she blessed me with items from her store. I enjoyed my time working for her.

Next, I got a job at a local restaurant. It was often not busy, so she would pack some of her food into takeaway containers and tell me to haul it to different shops across various parts of Southeast London. My customers were those working in barbershops and hairdressers. Often guys would patronize me just as an excuse to talk to me. I later left and began to work at another cab office in Peckham.

My then-boyfriend was also a married man. I became intimately involved with him for a period, regardless of the glaring red flags in our relationship. In hindsight, I feel he was either with me out of pity or leading me on, but that is not to say that I did not enjoy every bit of it at the time. I did. Eventually, I became pregnant for him and got an abortion.

Time passed, and a pattern emerged in my life. I would leave my dad's house at night and sometimes return the following morning. I believe this was part of the reason my dad asked me to leave his house.

I remember that day. He banged his hand on the table and said he wanted me out of the house. He was generous enough to give me an ultimatum, unlike my foster mum's brother, who arrived from the United States and threw us out without mercy.

The night I left, I remember I made my way to Morrison's in Peckham. Peckham is a busy multicultural area in London.

I agreed to meet a lady from whom I hoped to rent a room from. Shortly after arriving at Peckham, I was in tears because the lady I had decided to live with disappointed me in the end. She refused to answer my calls, leaving me stranded. I decided to find a place to sit, which I did, on the floor by the Morrison's grocery store. I was hoping something could happen to help me out. People walked by without a care in the world while I was in tears.

Fortunately, God sent a former colleague from the cab office where I worked to the place where I was sitting. It was an odd place, so it could only have been God who put him in my path. He saw me and was surprised. It was very late at night, with hardly anyone still around. After explaining what had happened, he took me back to the cab office and told others about my plight. Eventually, someone offered to rent me one of their spare rooms. That was how God saved me from sleeping on the street that night.

I also want to thank my old colleague for

allowing God to pass through him to help me. I followed him to the spare room and went to sleep shortly after. Despite my imperfection, I could not thank God enough for sending me timely help.

After several months of moving from one job to another, looking for something more, God answered my prayers and gave me a breakthrough. I got a cleaning job at a hotel with my friend's assistance. My friend from my former church was close to the manager of the cleaning department. While trying to get me the job, my friend was honest with the manager and explained that my papers had expired and that I was using someone else's documents. He recruited me nonetheless, and all was well at the beginning.

I settled in at the job and could afford to do my job with a cheerful smile. I was optimistic that from then on, things would only get better. Over time the manager of my department began to make advances on me. Eventually, the departmental manager was sacked. Not because of me but because one of the other female cleaners complained that he was making her feel uncomfortable with his sexually suggestive conduct.

He became angry with other members of staff

and me because he felt no one showed concern for him when he was sacked. He also threatened me that he would tell the hotel manager that my papers had expired. He eventually carried out his threat. The Hotel manager called me, questioning me about my papers. I confessed it to be true, and he said I should speak to him at the end of the shift. My heart sank to my stomach. I wasn't myself throughout that shift; I couldn't eat. The hotel manager did not sack me as the former departmental manager had expected. It was not exactly new to have some immigrants with expired papers doing menial jobs.

After some time, the hotel manager, too, began to make advances on me. I later learned it was not a new thing to have employers and managers take advantage of immigrants with expired papers. To a large extent, the immigrants are at their mercy, so with some threat, they get their way with the usually helpless immigrants. I was unhappy about this, but because I needed the job, or rather the money the job provided, I had no choice but to play along.

Things got a bit better for me. I could pay my bills, although I could not afford most of the things I wished to have. I usually get dressed at work on

Sunday mornings after my shift and go to church. Those on the upper floor often complimented me as I made my way out of the building. My colleagues were consistently impressed by my appearance going to church. One of my co-staffs said I should be working on the upper floor. I believe my Sunday appearance percolated the interest of staff and managers alike. One day as I was cleaning the office, one of the managers walked in and asked me if I was still comfortable cleaning or if I would like to come up and join them on the upper floor. I was elated, and my response was to join them. That's how I was promoted to the first floor within my workplace. Although I was grateful to God for my elevation at work. I couldn't help but be unsatisfied. I sensed a void within me, yearning to be filled. After all, it was still not the kind of life I had hoped for when I first arrived in the United Kingdom.

I made new friends and tried improving my lifestyle as best as possible. I was no longer a child at this period, so my reasoning had changed significantly over the years. One thing I cannot forget about that period in my life is the emptiness within my soul. I spent time with people, laughed, and cracked jokes, but I was always at the edge of depression. One of the reasons I spent so much time with others was because I needed the distraction from the reality of my life. As soon as I was on my own, it was as if darkness began to creep into my soul. Negative thoughts flood my soul, making me feel like a ship on the ocean without a rudder for direction.

Despite everything, I continued living my life daily, independent of my parents or anybody else. My job at the hotel paid relatively well and got me some relative comfort. I tried adjusting to the new life, but deep within me, I was still not happy or fulfilled.

Chapter 6

My Journey of Change

In 2016, one of my friends from my old church invited me to another church, Mountain of Fire and Miracles Ministries, for a 3-day fasting and prayers program. When he mentioned this, I was excited. I've had a good experience with this ministry back in Nigeria, so I was expectant that after this program, My Life would change. Also, owing to my life's direction, I obliged and went with him to the church. Things were not good for me, and I knew I needed help. I needed not to be told that how my life was shaping out could only lead me to a disastrous old age. The only problem was that I did not know who to turn to.

Most of the people I knew also had their issues to sort out. I realized that people were only willing to spend time with you if you keep your problems to yourself. As soon as you air your worries and challenges, they begin to avoid you. Some will even prey on you with your vulnerabilities, use you and end up compounding your problems. If someone was willing to help, it usually comes with a condition. You see, life in the UK isn't easy for the typical working person. Every pound usually matters significantly to them, and many barely live above water.

I managed to complete the intense three days of fasting and prayers. It was a herculean task at the time, but Holy Spirit helped me, and I could complete it without defaulting. After the three days of fasting and prayer, I felt different. It was as if something had changed, but I could not put my finger on it.

I went back to my church feeling like something was accomplished, and I was expectant that God was about to change my life.

I again completed their three-day fasting and prayers program the following month. A week later, I got a marriage proposal from my husband. It was amazing! I knew God would do something new in my life, but I never thought He would settle that area of my life so soon. I knew my husband. We had been friends, attending the same church for five years, and it was not until I completed this fasting and prayers that he came and proposed to me. It was as if his eyes opened, and he saw a different person in me. We eventually started the courtship process, which led to our wedding. Everything happened so fast, the chemistry, the willingness to weather the storm of life together; it was all so amazing. We are now happily married and have two beautiful children. Thank You, Jesus.

It was almost immediate when problems began to arise in our newly formed family. Our finances became extremely tight, and we began to beg whomever we could for assistance. There were times when we had no baby formula for our daughter, so we had to beg for money to buy it. There was even a time when I had a painful toothache, but there was no money to purchase pain relief medication. We were living from hand to mouth. We also had spiritual attacks. Things became so dire that I told my husband to look after our three-month daughter so I could go back to Mountain on Fire Ministries to attend their 3-day fasting and prayers program. However, when I got there, I was surprised that their monthly fasting and prayer program was not on and closed. So, I returned home disappointed and wondering what I would do next. Soon after, God brought the ministry I am now a member of on my path.

In 2017, I came across a woman of God preaching on Facebook; Apostle Belema Abili. A friend of mine shared her video on Facebook. I saw the video and was instantly drawn to her. I began to follow her; weeks later, God gave me the gift of speaking in tongues.

I continued to watch and follow Apostle Belema Abili, and I had a dream one night. In this dream, I saw a woman on a stage preaching with many people in the congregation watching her. I knew that it was Apostle Belema Abili. I was also in the congregation. Someone sitting close to me said, "I will use you the way I am using her." The dream was so vivid, and I shared it with my husband, who had been so supportive. I realized God was speaking to me through the woman of God, so I stayed connected and continued to watch her videos online.

I watched the woman of God video almost every day. They kept me company when my husband was at work all day. It helped keep my mind off our challenges and kept me going.

God gave my family and me breakthrough. I

participated in a 7-day dry fasting and prayers event with the woman of God, and God gave my husband a new and better-paid job. It was such a relief and much-needed intervention because we were faced with the possibility of moving back to my husband's mum's house because of our financial difficulties. This paved the way for us to move out and into a better place. God has used the woman of God as a channel of such great blessing to my family and me. The Lord has led her to bless us financially many times, equating to thousands of dollars. God also used her to give me my documents. This is a big deal. It was something that my husband and I couldn't do for lack of money. God provided and used her to bless us with $5000.

God also revealed to me that my biological mother is a witch! I know that seems unbelievable to you, reader, but it all started as a revelation from a dream. In the dream, I saw myself at a church programme hosted by my mother in the Lord Apostle Belema Abili. While on the stage, she called my mother by her native name in the audience. The apostle told her that she was a witch and was on a mission to initiate a young boy, but she would fail. In the dream, I saw my mother stand up from her chair in the congregation and confess, "I'm a witch, oh, I'm a witch, oh." She was touching her body as if an invisible fire was burning her.

In the dream, I told her I had always suspected her to be one, but I could not say it with certainty. My biological mother also confessed that my in-laws were witches. They had also failed in their assignment, so they were looking for an insider to complete their assignment, and she was the insider. She said they have been telling her to come to London, but she has been giving them excuses about her business. I asked her in the dream how she was planning to come to London without telling me, and she said she was just going to show up as a surprise.

The scene in the dream changed from a church auditorium to my house. I went to my husband and explained that my mum was a witch. I also saw my biological mother trying to give my husband something to eat, but I collected it from him. Furthermore, in the dream, I told my birth mother, "so does it mean that you're using your restaurant to cage people's glory." Then while she was still manifesting, I walked her out of my house and closed the door.

When I woke up, I thought it was only a dream. I never understood the meaning of the word "assignment" or "insider" within the context that I said in the dream. Not long after, I got several confirmations from other servants of God. Hallelujah!

Daniel 2:22 says, 'He revealeth the deep and secret things: he knoweth what is in the darkness, and the light dwelleth with him' (King James Version)

In 2019 I participated in 13 hours speaking in tongues event with my Apostle. Immediately after the event, Apostle Belema Abili said that God said that in three days, some of us watching her would receive something from Him or will have an encounter with Him. Even though the message was unclear to me, I did not know precisely how God would give me something, I believed, and eventually, it happened. On the third day, I had a dream. I saw a man sitting in an office. I was also in the man's office and approached him at his desk. He gave me a brown envelope; a piece of white paper could be seen sticking out at the top of the envelope. There was something written on the exposed part of the white paper in the envelope. I looked carefully to see what was written on the paper and read 'Amarachi's Ministries.

A third word was added to what was written, but I can't remember it. I then passed the envelope to my husband, and the dream ended. This was how I received the name of my ministry. This was a bit of a surprise to me. This was not something I was thinking about. I thought this was something I would do in the future. You see, I didn't have much bible knowledge at the time. I didn't know how to preach, nor did I have the confidence to address people in that capacity. I had no idea God placed me in the woman of God's ministry to learn for that purpose. Soon after, a man of God from Nigeria who was friends with my family member came to the UK and paid my husband and me a visit. He prophesied that God has put His power in me and prayed for us. Soon after, I began to do deliverance on my husband. The demons in him would manifest, and many things were said, but I was only doing this indoors, privately, and not in public.

One day Apostle Belema Abili posted on Facebook, *Matthew 5:16*; In the same way, let your good deeds shine out for all to see so that everyone will praise your heavenly Father (NLT). As I read this, I felt a fire in my heart. God began to speak to me.

He said that He has put a gift in me and that I should start using it, and when I start using it, people will see what He is doing through me and glorify Him. I started crying. I began saying; I do not know where to start preaching. Is it on the street, on Facebook, etc.? I also had low self-esteem. While growing up, people often made jest of me, saying I had four o clock or six o clock eyes, so often I struggled to maintain eye contact with people.

I was also very shy and could easily be intimidated. I could not speak fluent English, and my accent still reflects my African background. I reckoned that people would laugh at me. God went on to give me multiple confirmations through many of His servants. On the 5th of June 2019, God led me to preach my first message, "God's Love." I remember that after I began preaching, God gave me a message to Tell people about his love, preach salvation, and do healing and deliverance. He also said I should not preach financial prosperity messages. To the Glory of God, He has anointed me as His servant, and below are some testimonies of those God has touched through my ministry. But first, I would like to share this scripture with you from *Mark 16:20*;

"And they went forth, and preached everywhere, the Lord working with them, and confirming the word with signs following. Amen", King James Version:

A Few Testimonies

Sunitta Crandon
I feel relieved right away from the back pain, it was so bad, medication wasn't helping. Thank you very much appreciated.

Hannah Asobo
Woman of God since you prayed for my son he's more focused in his school work now. Thank You Jesus.

Testifier
Good morning sister. My daughter that was sick that you prayed for is fine now. Thank you for your prayer and I Thank God.

Susan Abraham
Thank you dear for praying for me. I've been truly blessed in my job. Praise The Lord! Alleluia Amen.

Chinasa Obi
God day woman of God. The midnight prayer in which we prayed against witchcraft or anything that is on an assignment to monitor me. That prayer was for me. I just killed a very big spider. Thank You Jesus.

Idyllic Lee Petra
You prayed for me last week and now my clinic is growing and I believe it will only get better. Thanks

Sumitta Shamshad
Last week I asked you to pray for me to get a job. Today I have received my appointment letter. Praise The Lord! Thank you. God bless you more.

David Cossey
My testimony is my bad dreams have gone. God bless you.

Hannah Asobo
Woman of God my blood pressure has been normal since you prayed for me. Thank You Jesus.

Tafadzwa Mparadzi
Thank you so much for the prayers yesterday. I had a terrible headache before but after the midnight prayer it's now much better. Now I am totally healed, it stopped now. Thank you, thank you.

Testifier
Hello woman of God, I appreciate God for your life and ministry. More grace and anointing woman of God. I want to give God The Glory and honour for the encounter I have had through watching the midnight prayer on 14th April 2020. I had deep yawns, teary eyes, a running nose and I coughed and burped through out while you were praying for us. Afterward I felt very cold all over and I even looked for socks to put on. I jumped into my bed to keep warm. I felt fire radiating on my head. It was like someone stood on my right-hand side and placed his hand on my head. I'm still feeling the heat up to now. To God Alone Be All The Glory And Honour. God bless you woman of God. More grace and anointing.

Tangeni David
I just realised that the stomach ache that I had is gone. I'm free now. To God Be The Glory.

Dorcas E
Mum good morning. The first day you prayed for me you mentioned my family. Your prayers are working for us. Our last born just got engaged yesterday. Thanks for your prayers may God bless you more and more.

Testifier
Woman of God after you prayed for me on your live video I had a dream I was killing a snake in the house and when he tried to hide inside the bed I pulled it outside and killed it. Thank you so much mum for your love and prayer.

Grace
Woman of God my miracles don start this morning when I woke up. I woke up to good news. I'm almost exploding with joy. Remember my friend, she delivered naturally this morning. I'm bubbling with joy. She gave birth to a beautiful baby boy. God bless you, He Honoured His Word.

Suzanne Mahfood
Praise God. Woman of God I always felt lazy to pray late in the night, but you had these midnight prayers. I started to stay up with you to pray, in fact I became addicted to stay up and pray with you. My family history is heart disease, and so I started having extreme pain day and night in my heart during the covid 19 pandemic. I was unable to go GP so one night I was joining in your midnight prayer, I had an episode and felt like I was not going to make it that night, so I message

you for prayer. You started to name all the things that was happening to me in that moment. It was so supernatural. My eyes were closed and immediately I saw a woman lying in a hospital bed and you came and took her hands and she raised up from the bed. Woman of God this is no joke from that very moment every pain left my chest it was my best sleep ever. To God Be The Glory. I have more testimonies I will send soon. God bless you.

Testifier
Good evening woman of God. I was feeling serious pains all over my body. After you prayed for me I got instantly healed. I want to Thank God for this healing and Thank God for you woman of God.

Jane
Thank You Jesus. I tapped into this deliverance. Oh my goodness I yawned uncontrollably, coughed and had a running nose and got teary eyed. I also burped twice after drinking the water you blessed. Thank You Jesus I am free. God bless you woman of God.

Destiny
Woman of God as you were praying for the servant of God I tapped into the prayer because in my dream I say someone put fake eye contacts on top of my supernatural eyes. Now my eyesight is brighter. Thank You Jesus. Thank you woman of God. God bless you mightily.

Chukwudi Oputa
Great woman of God I appreciate God's call on your life. Since you did deliverance on my wife and I a lot has changed. My wife is now on fire, I mean real fire. Also the connections I was looking for is coming gradually and my fire has increased. Things are really happening now. Thanks and God bless. I would like to also tell you, after reading your message I feel light, like some weight has lifted.

Testifier
Hello woman of God! A couple of weeks ago whilst browsing on my phone I found your teaching on how to raise a child. I watched a little bit but didn't comment. I was just coming home from work that morning so I fell asleep. Whilst I was asleep I saw you passing by and I held onto your feet and you touched my head. Your hand was very heavy and I fell down. I believe that you

delivered me from something and I will send my deliverance offering. Thank You Jesus and thanks woman of God.

Marcella Farias
Yesterday I had some strange feeling in my body and was bleeding. I didn't have olive oil so I decided to use water instead. After you blessed the water I drank it and I went to bed. When I woke up the bleeding was gone. Thank you woman of God. Blessings to you and your family. I'm much better now. Thank You God.

Kadran Bailey-Hart
Woman of God as you praying on the prayer line I was shaking and manifesting but now I feel free. Thank You Jesus!

Heavenly Gem
Woman of God as you were praying I was yawning and burping deeply with tears. Thank You Jesus.

Jane-Tony Mungufeni Bileru
Thank You Jesus. I yawned uncontrollably since I joined this broadcast. I coughed and burped

out loud when you prayed against attacks on our prayer life and witchcraft attacks. Thank You Jesus.

Osaru
Hay hay hay Jehovah the over do has done it ooooo. My friend we prayed for who has been afraid to take her nursing exam for over a year now has just called me to say that she just passed. Hay This God is too good ooooo To Him Be All The Glory oooo.

Andrea Hinds
I would like to testify of God's Goodness and To Him Be All The Glory. My daughter got her results from the two exams. She passed both. Thank you woman of God for your prayers.

Veronica Ida Tuominen
I want to testifiy for my daughter too. She passed her exams two days ago. Lord I give You All The Glory, You have done it again. Glory, glory, glory!

Testifier
Last time when my mother was not well I sent you a message. We were in great distress because

my mother had tested positive for covid. Her symptons were vomittting, loose motions, low BP and tiredness. After you assured me that my mum was healed within two days she was healed completely. Her health improved a lot. The covid vanished and her BP is normal. Thank God for the assurance and your wonderful prayer and ministry.

Testifier
Good morning woman of God. After you text me back I became pregnant the following month. I want to celebrate the grace of God upon you life. Thank You Jesus.

Testifier
Morning. Woman of God thanks for praying for me yesterday on your live video. I slept well. No attack I am free from the demons.

Testifier from Nigeria
I want you to help me Thank God. You prayed for me and somebody payed for a fairly used Keke for me to start working. It was three hundred thousand naira for the Keke that he gave me free of charge. Now I will no longer be idle this year. I'm happy woman of God, your prayer worked. Thank you very much. God bless you ma.

Ejike Kenneth
Since you prayed for me I'm no longer having nightmares.

Ariec Nix
I want to testify. You prayed for me to receive employment. God not only answered our prayers but he did it in the most powerful way. He has given me a job which fits with my ministry. Thank God and thank you for your prayers. I love you woman of God.

Esther Salmah Azaman
Thank you so much woman of God. After you prayed for my sister she got her healing instantly. Thank You Jesus.

Suzanne
Greetings woman of God in Jesus name. I used to feel pain on my head but since you prayed for me that feeling has gone. Hallelujah Jesus.

Mariam
God bless you woman of God. I just want to

testify to The Glory Of God for delivering me from spiritual husband, serpentine spirit and breast pain when you prayed for me yesterday. All those demons left me and went back to the pit of hell. Hallelujah hallelujah! Thank You Jesus for delivering me. I am free and my deliverance is permanent in Jesus mighty name. More grace and thank you for availing yourself to God's calling. Lord I cannot Thank You enough, I return all the praise and glory To You. Amen and Amen.

Precious
Woman of God when we were praying against witches, I had a revelation. When I was praying for my husband, I saw an old woman with a walking stick leave the ground. I also saw it leaving my husband. When I was praying for myself and my siblings I saw myself in my father's house and saw five dwarfs jump out of them.

Testifier
Good Afternoon woman of God. I Thank God, Ikenna is healed. Thanks and God bless you.

Esther S Azaman
Good day woman of God. God bless you for

coming up with this prayer line. This is my testimony from the prayer line. Two days ago I tapped into a prayer you were praying for a sister on your live video because I woke up with a sore on both legs. So I tapped into the prayer and woke up to find that I was completely healed with no signs of soreness. Secondly my bed used to feel like I had company. At night I can wake up to find myself at different positions on my bed. Since the night I tapped into your prayer my nights have been so peaceful. I wake up in the spots I slept off in. Thank You Jesus and thank you woman of God. My prayer life has been restored by this prayer line and I feel in my spirit that things are going to take a new turn in my life. God bless you ma'am for the good work. I will surely be back with more.

Testifier
Good evening woman of God. God bless you and your family. I have come to testify To The Glory Of God that John Okoh can now stand. I try and join whenever you are live but I have a phone challenge. More grace to you and your ministry. Thanks.

Diana S
You just prayed for me. You asked me if someone has prayed for me before and I said Pastor I.S

but I just remember that there is another Pastor that I met in my church. I asked him to pray for me last year and he told me he saw something in my private parts, and the only way for it to come out is for him to put his finger inside of me while he prays. I accepted this at the time because I respected him as a man of God until recently when I heard about false prophets. Oh God!! Is this what you saw?? He put something in me Oh Lord. After your prayer I'm feeling light and good. Thank You Jesus.

Amara
I spoke to you last year about not being in a stable relationship and not having a good job. I later got a good job in June last year and gave my testimony. You also told me that I would meet a good man that would get married to me. I want to return all The Glory To God. I met him in February this year and we just concluded our traditional wedding.

Testifier
Good day woman of God. You prayed for me against moving objects a week ago, and I must say the situation has drastically improved. I can now sleep peacefully. God Be Praised and I Thank Him for using you as His servant to set His children free. You are a true blessing and may God bless

you.

Akhona Samson
Woman of God I want to give my testimony. I asked you to pray for my brother Chumani and now he is discharged from the hospital. Thank you for your prayers and for allowing God to use you. Stay blessed.

Kathryn Korksey
Thank You Jesus. Woman of God I just want to testify. My son got into a car accident and suffered from third degree burns. Just wanted to let you know that after you prayed my son is now back at work. To God Be The Glory.

Janet M
Morning woman of God. I just want to give God Glory for what He has done. I asked you to pray for me to be able to read my bible and pray without falling asleep. I can confirm that God has done it for me. Glory Be To God. More grace unto you. Thank you so much.

Idyllic Ema J
Thanks woman of God for praying for me. I have

seen a little change in my business.

Carol M W
Hello. Praise Jesus. I have a testimony. The night before yesterday I received instant healing when you prayed for the sick. Glory Be To God and be blessed.

Floxy Topez
Praise The Lord. I have come to return all The Glory To God. God intervened. The company that owns the material asked my brother to write a report, which he did. He wasn't arrested nor asked to pay for the items as it couldn't be found. I am so happy for what God has done. May His Name only be glorified forever. Thank you woman of God for your prayers. May His anointing continue to increase upon your life. Amen.

Alice Solomon
Good afternoon woman of God. I sent you a message for prayer but you didn't respond. However, I had a dream that you were with one of my friend's and I told you that I sent you a message regarding stagnation and you laughed. You then delivered me from that spirit and led me out of a cage. Thank you so much, more grace

more anointing woman of God.

Astrude Roberts Nelson
Hi woman of God. After conducted my deliverance on your live video here is what I vomited.

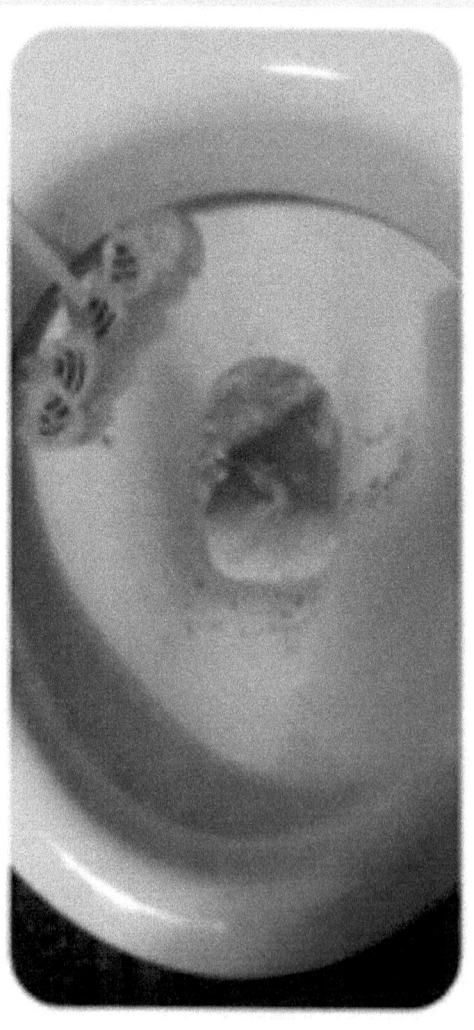

Chinasa Obi
Good evening woman of God. Here is my testimony. After you prayed for my son who has never walked since the day I gave birth to him, he is now walking with shoes.

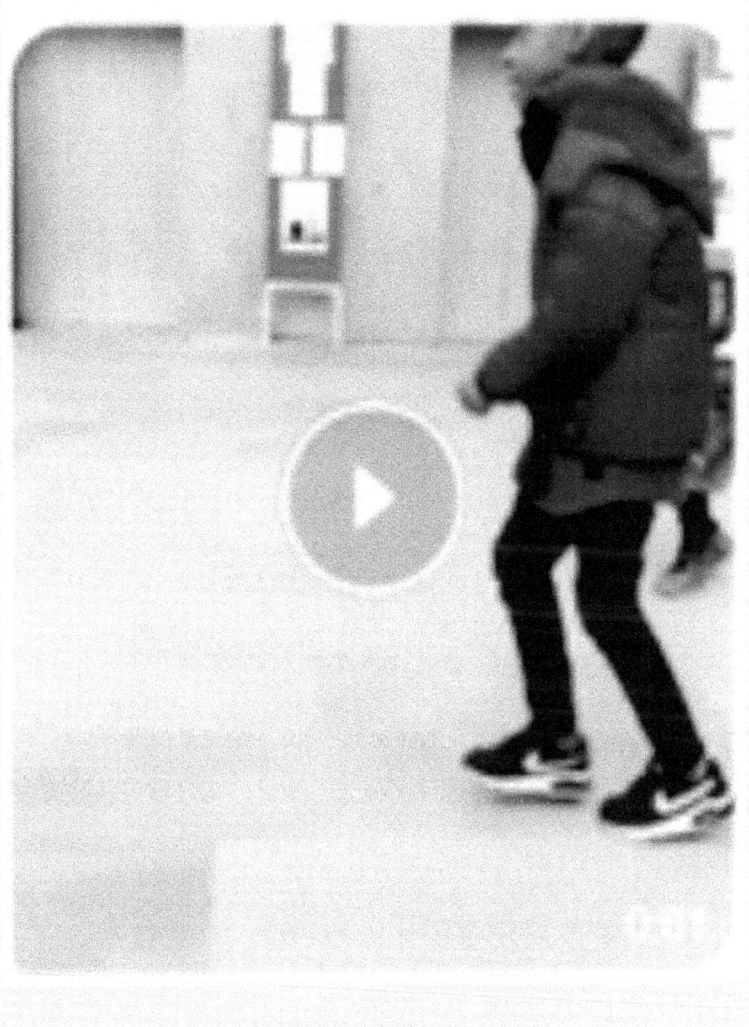

Abhi Gal
I sent you message at 1:34am Central Africa Time. I have been struggling to achieve anything since I graduated. I haven't got a job, im not married and I have been unsuccessful in business. Last year I fell sick and suffered from pains all over my body. I also suffer sleep paralysis and eat in my dreams. I would like to tell you that after reading your prayer message you typed I feel light like some weight has lifted.

Susan Abraham
You prayed for God to heal me from osteoarthritis. Thank You Jesus and thank you dear as the pain has eased off. Praise The Lord!

Tangeni David
Good day woman of God. I was having a pain in my throat and you prayed for me two weeks ago. Well the pain is gone and I'm totally healed. Glory Be To God.

Testifier from Africa
Praise Jesus. Woman of God after the prayer last week, I am happy and glad that the issue of urinating on my bed has improved.

To the Glory of God, the Lord Jesus has used me to win souls and bring major deliverance and healing to people's lives on social media and outside of social media. I give God all the Glory.

For the interactive prayer of healing and deliverance, message me at www.angelosisioma.co.uk.

Chapter 7

Stumbling into Destiny Fulfilment

The night is far spent, the day is at hand: let us, therefore, cast off the works of darkness, and let us put on the armor of light. *Romans 13:12 KJV*.

Many Christians today proclaim to belong to Christ but remain in darkness. They go to church, worship, and pray to God with seriousness, but unknown to them, they are still operating in the dark of night rather than in the light of day. No wonder *Isaiah 50:10 (KJV)* says: Who is among you that feareth the LORD, that obeyeth the voice of his servant, that walketh in darkness, and hath no light? Let him trust in the name of the LORD and stay upon his God. You may think you are upright in Christ but may be in darkness.

Another side to Christians walking in darkness has to do with cases where deep within you know you love and belong to God, but you still find yourself acting contrary to His will. I was like that once, but God delivered me and is helping me to fulfill my destiny. Even though I was walking in the darkness of confusion and indecision, the Holy Spirit guided my stumbling through the dark to my glory.

Darkness in this context can mean several things. It can be sin, a life devoid of the glorious light of the gospel of Christ, or a life spent running away from His call.

Sin, in this case, can be what the Bible calls presumption sin, meaning willful sin. This can be seen in *Psalms 19:13*, where the Bible says, "keep back thy servant also from presumptuous sins; let them not have dominion over me: then shall I be upright, and I shall be innocent from the great transgression." Those who engage in such sin are operating in the dark. I was like that once, but now I am in the light.

Sin here could also refer to the account in *Hebrews 12:1 (KJV)*: Wherefore seeing we also are compassed about with so great a cloud of witnesses, let us lay aside every weight, and the sin which doth so easily beset us, and let us run with patience the race that is set before us. You know that singular weakness you have, that sin you keep falling into. That sin is holding you in the dark, I had such in my life too once, but today I am totally delivered, Hallelujah!

The sin here could also mean ungodly acts done out of ignorance. Many of us still harbor some ungodly characters and activities out of ignorance; come out of that evil today and be saved. The good news is that the Bible assures us in *Acts 17:30 (KJV)* that "And the times of this ignorance God winked at, but now commandeth all men everywhere to repent." Also, in *Hebrews 8:12 (KJV)*, the Bible says, "for I will be merciful to their unrighteousness, and their sins and their iniquities will I remember no more."

A life without the light of Christ will remain in the darkness of confusion, all sorts of life challenges, and the devil's torments. Satan will always seek to blind the mind of men from receiving the light of Christ through the gospel so he can continue to control them. *2 Corinthians 4:4 (KJV)* states clearly that "In whom the god of this world hath blinded the minds of them which believe not, lest the light of the glorious gospel of Christ, who is the image of God, should shine unto them." A life without Christ is a life of crisis. Even if such men appear comfortable today, eternal torment still awaits them in hell. May that not be your portion in Jesus' name.

Also, running away from the call to give your life to Christ or accept to work for Him will only make such a person be in darkness. Jesus Christ is the light of the world and whoever runs away from light has only one place to go, and that is darkness. Jesus Christ said in *John 9:5 (KJV),* "As long as I am in the world, I am the light of the world." Therefore, running away from Jesus Christ is running away from light. For your light to shine to the whole world in destiny fulfillment, you must tarry long with the one who is the Light of the world.

You might have found yourself living a meaningless life. You might have been living a life without a clear-cut direction. Maybe you even know in your heart that you belong in the light of Christ, but somehow you are still in sin or the valley of indecision. I want you to know that God yet has a plan for you.

You may wonder why you are still struggling to find a purpose for living, but I want you to know today that with God, nothing happens for nothing. You may be stumbling in the dark today, but very soon, you are stumbling into your destiny fulfillment in Jesus' name.

Romans 8:28 (KJV) says, "And we know that all things work together for good to them that love God, to them who are the called according to his purpose." No matter what you are going through today, it is for your testimony to be complete; just believe! According to *Proverbs 16:9*, a man may plan his own way, and make his own decision, but it is the Lord who orders his steps. Whatever the place you are in life today, I see God ordering your step back in line in the mighty name of Jesus. He has ordered the steps of many in the past from the goriness of sin to the glory of righteousness and from a life of mess to a life of message.

An important fact you need to know is that even in your stumbling and seeming spiritual blindness God is at work because you are destined for great things. *Jeremiah 1:5 (KJV)* Before I formed thee in the belly, I knew thee; and before thou camest forth out of the womb I sanctified thee, and I ordained thee a prophet unto the nations. Between your birth and the fulfillment of your destiny in Christ, you may pass through many trials and unfortunate situations, but because God has a plan for you from your mother's womb, you will yet fulfill your destiny. *Psalms 34:19 (KJV)* says, "Many are the afflictions of the righteous: but the LORD delivereth him out of them all." Your afflictions may be much, and your path may seem difficult, but at the appointed time, God will show up for you.

However, that is not to say you should intentionally remain in the darkness of ignorance and sin once the truth is revealed to you. You must consciously find your way to the light by first accepting Christ as your Lord and personal savior. If you accept Him into your life, you receive the redeeming grace to become a child of God and joint heir with Christ Jesus. *John 1:12 (KJV)* says, "But as many as received him, to them gave He the power to become the sons of God, even to them that believe on His name." Something interesting that you will begin to experience is that His Spirit will bear witness with yours that you are indeed a child of God and joint heir with Christ Jesus. *Romans 8:15-17 (KJV)* For ye have not received the spirit of bondage again to fear; but ye have received the Spirit of adoption, whereby we cry, Abba, Father. The Spirit itself beareth witness with our spirit that we are the children of God:

And if children, then heirs; heirs of God, and joint heirs with Christ; if so be that we suffer with him, that we may be also glorified together. I decree concerning your life today that you will not remain in darkness. You will receive true sonship in God and fulfill destiny in Jesus' name.

There are examples in the Bible of people who stumbled into destiny fulfillment. We shall look at a few such people and how they made it through the darkness of life and still stumbled on to their destiny.

One of such examples of people in the Bible who stumbled through the darkness of uncertainty into their glory was David. When he was tending his father's sheep in the wilderness, he did not know that God had a big plan for his future. When he faced the dangers of lion and bear attacks, they were all part of God's plan for him. Then he faced Goliath and afterward found himself running for his life living in one cave. He became a fugitive and lived like a homeless vagabond, but he held unto his God all through those difficult fifteen years; he was stumbling into glory. He was stumbling to the throne of the kingdom of Israel.

Another good example was Joseph. He was his parent's favorite child and enjoyed that role until he was sold into slavery. Despite his dreams of ruling one day, his situation worsened, and he found himself in prison. At that point, it was no longer looking like there was a chance of him fulfilling his destiny, but the God who could reverse the irreversible reversed his situation and took him to the throne. After about fifteen years of stumbling in the valley of uncertainty, not knowing how God's revelations would come to pass, God still helped him fulfill his destiny. He stumbled through slavery and imprisonment but guess what? He made it to the door of destiny fulfillment. No matter how much you stumble today, your destiny shall not be truncated in Jesus' name.

Job also stumbled at some point in his life. He was rich and comfortable then it all went downhill for him. It was as if he was never going to rise again. He found his faith in God shaken and severely battered; he struggled through poverty, sickness, loss of children and properties, opposition from his friends, and discouragement from his wife. Through that stumbling period of his life, he never gave up, but at a point, he questioned God's reason for making such calamities befall him. However, the Bible records that God turned around his situation, and his latter end was better than the former; he still stumbled into his glory.

Job 42:10 (KJV) And the LORD turned the captivity of Job, when he prayed for his friends: also, the LORD gave Job twice as much as he had before.

Job 42:12 (KJV) So the LORD blessed the latter end of Job more than his beginning: for he had fourteen thousand sheep, and six thousand camels, and a thousand yoke of oxen, and a thousand she asses.

A few other biblical characters who struggled through dark times and mess into destiny fulfilling message include Rahab, who was a prostitute. She stumbled through the life of ignorance as a prostitute, but when destruction came upon Jericho, she was spared. She might have been a chronic sinner but stumbled to destiny fulfillment. Something unique about her is that even while in the darkness of ignorance, she recognized and acknowledged the power of God at work. Many people may be in the dark today but know and understand that Jesus Christ is Lord, yet they continue to struggle with sin. If you have faith today and call on Jesus to help you, you will overcome.

Hebrews 11:31 (KJV) By faith, the harlot Rahab perished not with them that believed not when she had received the spies with peace. Another interesting fact about Rahab is that she became the great-grandmother of our Lord Jesus Christ! What better way is there for her to fulfill her destiny? Even if you are a prostitute today, I decree that the grace to yet stumble into your destiny will fall on you in Jesus' name.

Mary Magdalene is another interesting character in the Bible who made it to destiny fulfillment despite her peculiar unpalatable situation. Several demons possessed her which may have led her to commit several sins.. Eventually, she met Christ, and her story changed for the best. No matter how many forces compete for authority over your life, the name of Jesus, which is more powerful than any evil force, set you free today. Receive Christ and be free forever.

An engaging portion of the Bible rings in my head whenever I think of destiny fulfillment. *Micah 7:8 (KJV)* Rejoice not against me, O mine enemy:

when I fall, I shall arise; when I sit in darkness, the LORD shall be a light unto me. You may be fallen today; you may be in the darkness of sin, confusion, poverty, indecision, demonic attack, homelessness, and so on; your enemies may be laughing you to scorn right now, but you will not remain there if only you will toe my path and find your way to Jesus Christ, my destiny helper. He will help you fulfill your destiny, and your story will change for the best.

Maybe you have been rejected by many in the past; I was also rejected several times; Christ Jesus is willing to receive you if only you accept Him. *Matthew 11:28 (KJV)* says, "Come unto me, all ye that labor and are heavy laden, and I will give you rest."

Finally, whatever the suffering you are experiencing today, I want you to remember that it is for your glory tomorrow. Decide for Christ today, turn your eyes to Him, and He will take you out of that path that can only lead to hell and place your feet on the path to destiny fulfillment. You are blessed in Jesus' name.

Chapter 8

Prayer Points

Tap into any of these prayer points that are relevant to you. If you believe it, God will touch you as you read. While he was still speaking to her, a messenger arrived from the home of Jairus, the leader of the synagogue. He told him, "Your daughter is dead. There's no use troubling the Teacher now. "But when Jesus heard what had happened, he said to Jairus, "Don't be afraid. Just have faith, and she will be healed." *Luke 8:49 – 50 KJV*.

- Anyone reading this book and believing God for a change in their life, receive it now in Jesus' name.

- Anyone sick in their body, be healed in Jesus' name.

- Anyone in any satanic cages, be released right now in the name of Jesus.

- Be free from any satanic operation, oppression, and attacks in Jesus' name.

- I pull you out from any marine kingdom you are in, in Jesus' name.

- Be free from any witchcraft coven in Jesus' name.

- I command every destructive moving object inside you to die in Jesus' name.

- Any satanic altar where your name is being mentioned, I command it to catch fire in Jesus' name.

- I cancel every blood covenant you are into in the name of Jesus.

- Receive your job now in Jesus' name.

- Receive the fruit of the womb in Jesus' name.

- Receive your papers and documents in Jesus' name.

- I cancel every spirit of rejection over your life in Jesus' name.

- I free your children from every satanic initiation in Jesus' name.

- Be restored now in Jesus' name.

- I release peace into your life now in Jesus' name.

- Receive favor all around, including your finances, in Jesus' name.

- I command anything that is not of God in you to come out in Jesus' name.

- If you haven't seen your period or the flow of your period is blocked or delayed, I unblock your period in the name of Jesus.

- I command your ears to be opened in the name of Jesus.

- I cancel every evil contract you have with the devil by the blood of Jesus.

- Every evil pattern occurring in your life and family, be destroyed now by the blood of Jesus Christ.

God can take you from where you are and change your life. He can make sense of a mess and turn it into a testimony because nothing is too hard for him to do. When God saved me, I was just like many of you. My life seemed hopeless. In Nigeria, I contemplated prostitution at one point because everything had crashed, and I needed the means to look after myself. My then-boyfriend dissuaded me not to take it up, demonstrating that God was not in my thoughts. Then one day, the unbelievable happened. God sent someone to help me even though I never deserved it. In my sin, my biological mother, who was told I had died, located me. In the UK, things did not turn out the way I expected. I became unhappy and entered a relationship with a married man. Again, God's mercy found me when I did not deserve it. He brought me into marriage and soon after into ministry to work for Him.

  I was molested. I began sleeping with men from a young age and often enjoyed it. I entered sexual relations with girls, engaged in pornography and masturbation, and even got involved in incest. This was the devil's handiwork. He sought to destroy me and put the spirit of lust in me. Yet God saved me, and he can save you. I cannot judge anyone because my track record makes me no better than you. I understand that your situation may have led you into the bad stuff you are doing. I understand that you may be doing what you are now doing to survive. Some of you are practicing witchcraft and need to repent. Some of you are engaging in lesbianism as I did. Some of you practice homosexuality, God can deliver you from it all. I am introducing Jesus to you because He can help you just as He helped me. Jesus loves you so much.

John 3:16 says, "For God so loved the world, that he gave his only begotten Son, that whosoever believeth in him should not perish, but have everlasting life" King James version.

He loves you, so why wouldn't He save you from your situation? However, you first must accept Him as your Lord and personal savior by confessing your sins and believing in His Son. Before I lead you down that road, I want to share a dream about Rapture.

Rapture is an event when those who have accepted Jesus as their Lord and Saviour and follow

Him obediently will be taken unexpectedly to heaven. *Matthew 24:30 – 31 NLT*:

And then, at last, the sign that the Son of Man is coming will appear in the heavens, and there will be deep mourning among all the peoples of the earth. And they will see the Son of Man coming on the clouds of heaven with power and great glory. And he will send out his angels with the mighty blast of a trumpet, and they will gather his chosen ones from all over the world—from the farthest ends of the earth and heaven.

One night while I was asleep, I had a dream. I saw many people, some in a choir and others in the world, going about their daily lives. Some were going to school while others were working in their businesses. Suddenly, at the speed of light, I saw some people in the choir being taken to heaven while others were left behind. I also saw some people in the world who were taken into heaven while others were left behind. The people who did not make it to heaven were crying bitterly, and, in the dream, it looked like I never made it. However, later I saw myself in heaven. I saw a man with a crown on his head. I couldn't tell the person's nationality, but

I believe this was Jesus. I also saw in the dream a gigantic hand. I was standing in between the left and right hand. The hands seemed like it was bigger than the whole earth. I could not see the man's face or body. The hands opened as if it was gesturing to the people welcome. Then I heard a voice. It was very deep, loud, and thundered, 'my children, you are welcome home.' The voice bid them welcome as the people were strolling into heaven. I noticed that they were so few. I remember seeing some people I knew in real life not making it to Heaven.

I realized that only a small percentage of people made it to Heaven. I believe God gave me that dream because He wanted me to pass on this warning to the world. What is more important is that you make it to heaven. You and I cannot afford to miss heaven. I've had several dreams like this one. However, all were slightly different. Jesus is coming back very soon. Then shall two be in the field; the one shall be taken, and the other left. Two women shall be grinding at the mill; the one shall be taken, and the other left. Watch therefore: for ye know not what hour your Lord doth come. *Matthew 24:40 – 42 KJV.*

If you would like Jesus to come into your life,

I want you to speak this prayer out of your mouth, believing with all your heart:

Heavenly Father. I come into Your Presence as a sinner. Please forgive me of all my sins. Today I ask that you be The Lord and Saviour of my life. Wash me with your precious blood. I promise by the help of The Holy Spirit to live to please you in Jesus's precious name; I pray. Amen.

Chapter 9

Conclusion

Genesis 50:20 reported when Joseph forgave His brothers for doing evil to him by selling him into slavery. It reads, "But as for you, ye thought evil against me; but God meant it unto good, to bring to pass, as it is this day, to save many people alive." In my case, the devil wanted to kill and destroy my life using the habits and sins I have highlighted in this book.

I remember my foster mum telling me a story. She said that when I was very young, I fell terribly sick as if I was going to die. My foster mum had a tenant who she later discovered was practicing witchcraft at that time. Mama confronted her one day and told her that she was a witch and demanded that she undo whatever she did to me. Suddenly, the woman began to pull her hair out, chew it, and confess that she was a witch. My foster mum then pinned her down and continued to demand that she undo whatever she had done to me. The tenant agreed and then proceeded to perform the ritual to undo the affliction she had put on me.

I believe God had done something to her that day and saved my life. Many years later, the tenant moved out and visited us. Mama repeated the story and told it to me in front of the former tenant. Mama was so fearless. The tenant affirmed it to be true, saying she did those things back then, but now she has repented and is a born-again Christian.

You see, the devil knew that God was going to use me, and he tried in many ways to kill me, but God never allowed it because He had a purpose for me.

The devil sought to destroy me, but Jesus saved me and made my story a testimony. He turned it around for good, and I can confidently tell you that Jesus will turn your situation into your testimony for His Glory in Jesus' name.

You see, God can do exceedingly abundantly above all that we can ask or think *(Ephesians 3:20 KJV)*. Seek him today. Seek ye first the kingdom of God, and his righteousness; and all these things shall be added unto you. *Matthew 6:33 KJV*.

A Letter of Thanksgiving to God

I want to thank my Heavenly Father for all He has done for me. As I mentioned, I wanted to go into prostitution to make a living. God came and rescued me offering me a much better life. It is written that Jesus came 'that they might have life, and that they might have it more abundantly' *John 10:10 KJV*. This is now undoubtedly the case with me. Thank you, Jesus, for rescuing me. God fought for me when I was a sinner and did not know Him. He made me invaluable to my biological mother, who left me as a baby and forgot about me.

She got married and tried for more children, but God closed her womb and pestered her with dreams about a child crying and holding unto her clothes. She came looking for me, being compelled by Him. God gave me my own husband and family when before that, I was just a lover to an already married man who had his own family. God anointed and ordained me as His servant. *Jeremiah 1:5 KJV* 'Before I formed thee in the belly, I knew thee; and before thou camest forth out of the womb I sanctified thee, and I ordained thee a prophet unto the nations. Thank you so much, Lord Jesus, for all you have done for me. Thank you for the undying love and mercy you have shown me.

Here I want to thank the instrument God has used to bring me into my purpose and calling. Her name is Apostle Queen Belema Abili of Queen Belemzy Ministries, School of Power. God has used her to teach me His Word and bring such invaluable wisdom into my life. The Bible says that 'Wisdom is the principal thing' *Proverbs 4:7 KJV*. Even with the anointing, you cannot be successful in ministry without wisdom and character. How would I be able to navigate the dangerous waters that are out there when in the field for God? God has used her openness and honesty to inspire me and make me more confident to open up to others about the uncomfortable truths in my past to help others.

Now I have the boldness to be on TV to preach The Gospel of Jesus Christ. She has been such a financial blessing to my life. My family and I were in severe financial difficulty. God used her to bless me with money many times, and through her, God has opened my financial doors. She also prophesied that I would be writing this book; today, that prophecy has been fulfilled by your reading this. Thank you so much, my mother in the Lord, Apostle Queen Belemzy, for allowing God to use you as my destiny helper. May the Lord take you from strength to greater strength in Jesus' name. Amen.

I would love to hear from you and know how this book has inspired or blessed you. Visit my website: www.angelosisioma.co.uk to send me a message. You can also send me a message via email: amarachisministries@gmail.com.

"Let your light so shine before men, that they may see your good works, and glorify your Father which is in heaven." **Matthew 5:16 KJV.**

About the Author

Amarachi Angel Osisioma Alaike is the steward of Amarachi's Ministries. She is a television evangelist whose sermons reach up to 45 million homes across the globe. She started preaching on social media, and God has used her mightily to heal and deliver many people with the evidence of testimonies that can be seen on her website and social media handles. She has also been used to touch lives on the streets of the United Kingdom. She is married to her husband, Victor Alaike, and she is blessed with two lovely children, Grace and David. Be sure to visit Angelosisioma.co.uk.

www.ingramcontent.com/pod-product-compliance
Lightning Source LLC
Chambersburg PA
CBHW041130110526
44592CB00020B/2746